Major US Historical Wars

The Vietnam War

Earle Rice Jr.

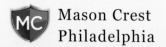

Mason Crest
Philadelphia

Mason Crest
450 Parkway Drive, Suite D
Broomall, PA 19008
www.masoncrest.com

Printed and bound in the United States of America.

CPSIA Compliance Information: Batch #MUW2015. For further information, contact Mason Crest at 1-866-MCP-Book.

3 5 7 9 8 6 4 2

Library of Congress Cataloging-in-Publication Data

ISBN: 978-1-4222-3359-7 (hc)
ISBN: 978-1-4222-8599-2 (ebook)

Major US Historical Wars series ISBN: 978-1-4222-3352-8

About the Author: Earle Rice Jr. is the author of more than 60 books. He served honorably in the U.S. Marine Corps as an infantry unit leader for nine years. Earle is listed in *Who's Who in America* and is a member of the Society of Children's Book Writers and Illustrators, the League of World War I Aviation Historians, the United States Naval Institute, the Air Force Association, and the Disabled American Veterans.

Picture Credits: Everett Historical: 42; Library of Congress: 13, 37, 39; Lyndon B. Johnson Library photo: 29, 31, 33, 47, 48; National Archives: 16, 17, 21, 23, 27, 34, 41, 44, 49, 53; Nixon Presidential Library and Museum: 52, 55; OTTN Publishing: 24; used under license from Shutterstock, Inc.: 10, 11; U.S. Air Force photo: 9, 26, 35, 50, 54; U.S. Army photo: 1, 7, 40; U.S. Marine Corps photo: 45; U.S. Navy photo: 32; Vietnam: 15, 19.

Table of Contents

KEY ICONS TO LOOK FOR:

Words to Understand: These words with their easy-to-understand definitions will increase the reader's understanding of the text, while building vocabulary skills.

Sidebars: This boxed material within the main text allows readers to build knowledge, gain insights, explore possibilities, and broaden their perspectives by weaving together additional information to provide realistic and holistic perspectives.

Research Projects: Readers are pointed toward areas of further inquiry connected to each chapter. Suggestions are provided for projects that encourage deeper research and analysis.

Text-Dependent Questions: These questions send the reader back to the text for more careful attention to the evidence presented there.

Series Glossary of Key Terms: This back-of-the book glossary contains terminology used throughout this series. Words found here increase the reader's ability to read and comprehend higher-level books and articles in this field.

Other Titles in This Series

Introduction

By Series Consultant
Lt. Col. Jason R. Musteen

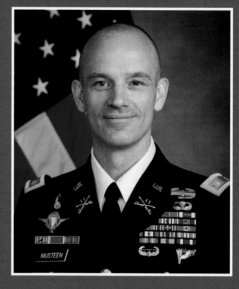

Lt. Col. Jason R. Musteen is a U.S. Army Cavalry officer and combat veteran who has held various command and staff jobs in Infantry and Cavalry units. He holds a PhD in Napoleonic History from Florida State University and currently serves as Chief of the Division of Military History at the U.S. Military Academy at West Point. He has appeared frequently on the History Channel.

Why should middle and high school students read about and study America wars? Does doing so promote militarism or instill misguided patriotism? The United States of America was born at war, and the nation has spent the majority of its existence at war. Our wars have demonstrated both the best and worst of who we are. They have freed millions from oppression and slavery, but they have also been a vehicle for fear, racism, and imperialism. Warfare has shaped the geography of our nation, informed our laws, and it even inspired our national anthem. It has united us and it has divided us.

Valley Forge, the USS *Constitution*, Gettysburg, Wounded Knee, Belleau Wood, Normandy, Midway, Inchon, the A Shau Valley, and Fallujah are all a part of who we are as a nation. Therefore, the study of America at war does not necessarily make students or educators militaristic; rather, it makes them thorough and responsible. To ignore warfare, which has been such a significant part of our history, would not only leave our education incomplete, it would also be negligent.

For those who wish to avoid warfare, or to at least limit its horrors, understanding conflict is a worthwhile, and even necessary, pursuit. The American author John Steinbeck once said, "all war is a symptom of man's failure as a thinking animal." If Steinbeck is right, then we must think. And we must think about war. We must study war with all its attendant horrors and miseries. We must study the heroes and the villains. We must study the root causes of our wars, how we chose to fight them, and what has been achieved or lost through them. The study of America at war is an essential component of being an educated American.

Still, there is something compelling in our military history that makes the study not only necessary, but enjoyable, as well. The desperation that drove Washington's soldiers across the Delaware River at the end of 1776 intensifies an exciting story of American success against all odds. The sailors and Marines who planted the American flag on the rocky peak of Mount Suribachi on Iwo Jima still speak to us of courage and sacrifice. The commitment that led American airmen to the relief of West Berlin in the Cold War inspires us to the service of others. The stories of these men and women are exciting, and they matter. We should study them. Moreover, for all the suffering it brings, war has at times served noble purposes for the United States. Americans can find common pride in the chronicle of the Continental Army's few victories and many defeats in the struggle for independence. We can accept that despite inflicting deep national wounds and lingering division, our Civil War yielded admirable results in the abolition of slavery and eventual national unity. We can celebrate American resolve and character as the nation rallied behind a common cause to free the world from tyranny in World War II. We can do all that without necessarily promoting war.

In this series of books, Mason Crest Publishers offers students a foundation for the study of American wars. Building on the expertise of a team of accomplished authors, the series explores the causes, conduct, and consequences of America's wars. It also presents educators with the means to take their students to a deeper understanding of the material through additional research and project ideas. I commend it to all students and to those who educate them to become responsible, informed Americans.

Chapter 1

Roots of the Vietnam War

From 1947 until 1991, the world's two most powerful countries, the United States and the Union of Soviet Socialist Republics (Soviet Union, or USSR), were locked in a tense, high-stakes conflict. It was known as the Cold War. The Cold War was not really a war in the way people typically use that term. The armed forces of the United States and the Soviet Union didn't fight each other directly. Instead, the Cold War is best understood as a political struggle—albeit one that was extremely wide ranging. The United States and the

The Vietnam War, in which American soldiers were engaged from the late 1950s until 1973, was different from past conflicts. U.S. troops found it hard to tell friend from foe, and their enemy struck quickly and then vanished into the jungle. These American soldiers are looking for communist-supported guerrillas known as the Vietcong.

Soviet Union battled for influence across the globe. They sought to enlist other countries as allies or, at the very least, to discourage other countries from siding with their adversary. The superpowers' confrontation played out in various arenas—military, economic, diplomatic, and even cultural.

The American system of liberal democracy emphasized individual rights and freedoms. These included political rights (such as the right to vote or run for public office) and civil rights (such as freedom of speech, the right to assemble peaceably, and freedom of the press). Americans were free to own businesses, run them the way they wanted to, and acquire all the personal wealth they could—a system called capitalism.

The Soviet system was underpinned by a theory called *communism*. It held that capitalism inevitably led to the exploitation of workers. Communists encouraged workers to revolt against their governments. They promised that under communism, everyone would be treated equally and each person would receive what he or she needed. The state would own factories and other places of work. It would run the economy not for the profit of individuals but for the benefit of all.

 ## WORDS TO UNDERSTAND IN THIS CHAPTER

communism—a political and economic system that champions the elimination of private property, promotes the common ownership of goods, and typically insists that the Communist Party has sole authority to govern.

ideology—a system of ideas and ideals, especially one that forms the basis of a political theory, such as democracy or communism.

in absentia—a Latin term meaning "in the absence." This is a legal term that refers to the conviction and sentencing of a person who is not present at the trial.

nationalism—the desire by a people who share a language and culture to gain a politically independent state of their own.

Vietminh—a contraction of *Vietnam Doc Lap Dong Minh*, meaning "League for Vietnamese Independence." This political organization was formed to fight for Vietnamese independence.

During the Cold War, the Soviet Union and other communist countries like China wanted to spread this *ideology* throughout the world. Leaders in the United States saw communism as a threat to their way of life, and wanted to keep it from spreading. The were willing to send money, weapons, and even American soldiers to support governments that opposed the spread of communism, even when those governments were not democratic or treated their people poorly. One place where the struggle between communists and anticommunists played out was Vietnam.

The Road to War in Vietnam

The roots of the American war in Vietnam go back to the late 1940s, just after the end of World War II. At that time, this part of Southeast Asia was a French colony known as Indochina. France had gained control over the region, which also included Laos and Cambodia, through a series of wars between 1859 to 1885.

Vietnam itself was partitioned into three territories: Tonkin, Annam, and Cochin China. Tonkin and Annam were protectorates. As such, they were administered by local officials, who reported to French authorities. Cochin China was a colony, ruled directly by French officials. The Vietnamese people did not wish to live under the rule of a foreign power, and they soon began to resist French policies.

In 1890, five years after France consolidated its colonies in French Indochina, a boy was born in the village of Hoang Tru in Nghe An

This map shows the colony of French Indochina, which included present-day Laos and Cambodia as well as the three territories that make up present-day Vietnam: Tonkin, Annam, and Cochin China.

province. His parents named him Nguyen Sinh Cung. He would later take many different names. During the 20th century, the world would come to know him best as Ho Chi Minh, meaning "Bringer of Light" or "Enlightener."

Ho received his formal education at the Quoc Hoc School in Hué, then spent much of his early life traveling the world. After serving as a cook on a French steamer for two years, he came to the United States in 1911. He worked at odd jobs in Boston, San Francisco, and New York, before moving on to London for two years. During World War I, Ho moved to Paris, where he worked as a gardener, a waiter, and at other unskilled labors. While there he met other Vietnamese living in France and became interested in politics.

During 1919, Paris was the site of a major peace conference that ended World War I. Before the war ended, U.S. president Woodrow Wilson had issued a document known as the Fourteen Points, which would be used as a basis for the peace agreements. One of Wilson's key points was that the boundaries of countries should be determined on the basis of *nationalism*. During the conference, the victorious Allied Powers (particularly the United States, Great Britain, France, and Italy) broke up the German, Austro-Hungarian, and Ottoman empires, creating many new countries based on the nationalities of people living in those territories.

Ho attended the conference along with other Vietnamese nationalists.

Vietnamese peasants harvest rice in the Mekong delta region. Most Vietnamese were poor farmers who lived on the food they produced. The Vietnamese peasants had been exploited for years by French colonial authorities and a wealthy landowning class. The peasants overwhelmingly supported the Vietminh and the communists, because they were willing to distribute the land among the people more fairly.

They wanted to meet with the Allied leaders, hoping that Vietnam could have greater freedom, as well as representation in the French parliament. However, the Vietnamese proposals were ignored or dismissed.

While in France, Ho became a member of the French Communist Party on December 30, 1920. French authorities began to keep a watchful eye on him as he studied the writings of Karl Marx and grew ever more active in anticolonial movements.

In 1923, Ho Chi Minh left Paris for Moscow, where he took an active part in the Comintern, an association of national communist parties dedicated to promoting world revolution. While in Moscow, he studied at the Communist University of the Toilers of the East and continued his active role in political affairs. He became acquainted with many communist leaders, including the future Chinese foreign minister Zhou Enlai.

The driving force behind Vietnam's 30-year fight for independence and, later, unity under a communist regime, Ho Chi Minh (1890–1969) was the founder of the Indochina Communist Party and president of the Democratic Republic of Vietnam (North Vietnam) from 1945 until 1969.

Although steeped in communist doctrine, Ho's underlying aim was national independence for Vietnam, not class warfare or other concerns of communism. Ho was a communist because he believed it to be the best available means to achieve Vietnamese independence from France.

Moving on to Canton, China, in 1924, Ho Chi Minh involved himself in Chinese communist activities and organized Vietnamese revolutionaries. In 1930, he founded the Indochina Communist Party (ICP). He began to recruit lieutenants and organizers, as well as rank-and-file members. Although the ICP was only one of several political parties and factions in Vietnam, it was, according to Ho, "the best organized and most active of them all."

Conflict in Indochina

The birth of the ICP coincided with a wave of harsh repressions by the French in Indochina. During the 1930s, French colonial authorities imprisoned and executed many of Ho's compatriots, condemning Ho himself *in absentia* to death as a revolutionary. Ho fled via Shanghai to Moscow to escape their sentence. He stayed there, studying and remaining politically active, until his return to China in late 1938.

In the little village of Lu Ma, outside Guilin in the heart of Guangxi province, Ho worked as a journalist and public health inspector. From his temporary base in south China, he carefully monitored the changes taking place in Indochina, particularly after World War II broke out in Europe in September 1939. When Germany defeated France in June 1940, Ho and his chief lieutenants, Vo Nguyen Giap and Pham Van Dong, plotted to use the fall of France to advance their quest for Vietnamese independence.

"The French defeat represents a very favorable opportunity for the Vietnamese revolution," Ho Chi Minh told his compatriots. "We must seek every means to return home to take advantage of it. To delay would be harmful to the revolution."

In January 1941, Ho and his lieutenants crossed over the border into Indochina and set up a base camp at Pac Bo. In May 1941, Ho, his two lieutenants, and five others formed the League for Vietnamese Independence, or *Vietminh*. The founding of this party brought renewed emphasis to the uniquely peasant-oriented Vietnamese brand of nationalism.

Ho warned his fellow revolutionaries about the hard road ahead. "Between the enemy and ourselves," he said, "it is a struggle to the death. We must be able to tolerate all hardships, surmount the worst difficulties, and struggle to the end." Ho's difficulties came sooner than expected.

After the conquest of France, Germany supported a puppet government set up at Vichy. The Vichy government continued to administer French colonies, including Indochina. It allowed Germany's ally, Japan, to operate from Southeast Asia as it attacked and conquered other countries and colonies in the region.

In August 1941, having established his internal program, Ho turned his attention to raising international support for his cause. China seemed like a good place to start, as it had been fighting against the Japanese since the mid-1930s. However, Ho's attempt to gain support from the Nationalist government of Chiang Kai-shek proved ill advised. Chiang had been fighting a civil war against Chinese communists for many years. He did not trust the Vietnamese leader because of his communist ties, and had him arrested. Ho spent the next 18 months in Chinese prisons. He gained release only after agreeing to support Chiang's interests in Indochina against the French.

Another country was more helpful: the United States. During the early years of the war the Vietminh had rescued American pilots who were shot down over the region, and helped them to escape Japanese capture and return to safety in China. In 1944, the Vietminh agreed to collaborate with the U.S. Office of Strategic Services (OSS). This American organization was the forerunner of the Central Intelligence Agency (CIA). For the remainder of World War II, the Vietminh fought a guerrilla war against the Japanese in Indochina and China. They spied on the Japanese, and used sabotage to prevent them from moving into China. In return, the Americans provided weapons and money.

During the spring of 1945, Vietminh guerrillas led by Vo Nguyen Giap and directed by Ho began advancing on Hanoi, the capital of French Indochina. They entered Hanoi on August 19, five days after Japan surrendered to Allied forces. Ho persuaded the French-supported emperor of

Leaders of the Allied countries—British prime minister Winston Churchill, U.S. president Harry S. Truman, and Soviet leader Josef Stalin—met at Potsdam, Germany, in July 1945. At the Potsdam Conference, the leaders agreed to temporarily partition Vietnam at the 17th parallel, just north of Da Nang. British forces would have authority for the southern zone, based in Saigon, while Chinese forces would control the northern zone, based in Hanoi.

Vietnam, Bao Dai, to abdicate the throne and allow the Vietminh to rule the country.

On September 2, the day on which Japan formally surrendered in Tokyo Bay, Ho appeared before a mass gathering in Hanoi's Ba Dinh Square. He proclaimed the independence of Vietnam and the establishment of the Democratic Republic of Vietnam. In his speech, he quoted from the U.S. Declaration of Independence, as well as the French Declaration of the Rights of Man. Ho also said, "We are convinced that the Allied nations, which at Tehran and San Francisco have acknowledged the principles of self-determination and equality of nations, will not refuse to acknowledge the independence of Vietnam."

The French Return

In return for supporting the interests of the Allied Powers (the United States, Soviet Union, Great Britain, France, and China) against the Japanese during World War II, Ho Chi Minh expected the Allies to support Vietnamese independence. He especially looked to the United States for affirmation. However, the Democratic Republic of Vietnam lasted only a few days. At the Potsdam Conference in July–August 1945, the Allies had decided that China and Great Britain would jointly occupy Vietnam to supervise the disarmament and repatriation of Japanese forces. For the foreseeable future, Ho Chi Minh's government effectively ceased to exist.

The Allied powers, particularly Great Britain, did not want to see colonial empires broken up after World War II, as they had been after the First World War. Britain had a worldwide network of colonies, and would be weakened significantly if they gained independence. France too was determined to reassert its influence and maintain its colonial interests in Indochina.

The United States, meanwhile, was experiencing a rift between its former ally, the Soviet Union. The Soviets were threatening to expand their communist ideology throughout Europe. U.S. policymakers recognized that they needed France's help to contain the spread of communism. Thus they were willing to support the French effort to regain control of its Indochina colony. Faced with the loss of outside support, Ho Chi Minh and his followers were forced to reconsider their approach.

During 1946, Ho Chi Minh tried to negotiate political independence for Vietnam. One agreement called for recognition of the Democratic Republic of Vietnam as a "free state" associated with France. However, difficulties arose at once over the flawed agreement, which did not precisely define the new state. The Vietnamese interpreted the new state to consist of Tonkin, Annam, and Cochin China. But the French gave no sign of recognizing any single government to rule over the three Vietnamese regions of their Indochina colony. Details of the new state's relationship to France also went undefined.

The First Indochina War Begins

At a subsequent conference in Paris during September 1946, Ho Chi Minh was asked to sign another agreement. This one was intended to facilitate the resumption of French economic and cultural activities in Vietnam. In return, the French government promised to introduce a more liberal colonial regime. However, the September agreement did not include any recognition of Vietnamese unity or independence. This omission raised a red flag and dissent among Ho's followers. French actions to implement customs controls aroused further hostility in October 1946. In November, shooting broke out in Hanoi's port city of Haiphong. French tanks, aircraft, and naval guns bombarded the city, killing as many as 6,000 Vietnamese.

On December 17, 1946, members of the Vietminh militia killed three French soldiers in Hanoi. That evening, General Vo Nguyen Giap made what amounted to a declaration of war: "I order all soldiers and militia in the center, south and north to stand together, go into battle, destroy the invaders, and save the nation. . . . The resistance will be long and arduous, but our cause is just and we will surely triumph." The people of Vietnam braced themselves for another long conflict, now called the First Indochina War.

During the early months of 1947, French forces regained control of the principal towns in Tonkin

Vo Nguyen Giap was the top military commander of the Vietminh and, later, of the North Vietnamese Army.

A French Foreign Legionnaire walks along the edge of a rice paddy during a sweep through communist-held areas between Haiphong and Hanoi. Behind the Legionnaire is a tank provided to French forces by the United States.

and Annam and cleared the road from Haiphong to Hanoi. French control of the population centers forced the Vietminh into the outlying areas. In the rural areas they reverted to the guerrilla tactics that had proved so effective against the Japanese. Their "hit-and-run" tactics neutralized the mechanized mobility and firepower of their enemy. French soldiers, trained in more conventional types of warfare, could not cope with the Vietminh's brand of "shadow" warfare.

After three years of fighting, the military situation remained pretty much unchanged. The French controlled the large cities; the Vietminh commanded much of the countryside. Politically, however, two competing Vietnamese governments emerged. One was Ho Chi Minh's Democratic Republic of Vietnam (DRV), based in the north. The other was the

Republic of Vietnam, headed by the former emperor Bao Dai and support-ed by the French government. It was based in the south.

Early in 1950, China became the first state to recognize the Democratic Republic of Vietnam as the legitimate government of all Vietnam. The Soviet Union and other communist countries followed suit soon after-ward. In February 1950, Great Britain and the United States countered by recognizing Bao Dai's regime as Vietnam's legitimate government.

The American Commitment Begins

On June 25, 1950, the communist forces of North Korea, supported by China, invaded South Korea. President Truman, without waiting for the U.S. Congress to act, committed troops to aid South Korea under the aus-pices of the United Nations. To policymakers in Washington, D.C., North Korea's aggression marked a turning point in Asia. They saw the fight for independence in Vietnam as another example of communist expansion-ism directed by Beijing and Moscow.

On July 26, 1950, President Truman signed legislation authorizing $15 million in military aid to the French for their war in Indochina. The United States had officially chosen sides in the struggle.

In 1951, the French military tem-porarily halted the advance of Vietminh forces with the aid of U.S.-supplied equipment. The next year, however, the communists launched a new offensive from several locations. Vigorous French counterattacks suc-ceeded only in maintaining a military standoff.

By 1954, the United States had supplied 300,000 small arms and machine guns and spent $1 billion in support of French military efforts in Indochina. Put another way, the United States—through the adminis-tration of President Dwight D.

French soldiers question a suspected Vietminh guerrilla captured in the jungle, circa 1954.

Eisenhower, Truman's successor—was footing the bill for nearly 80 percent of France's war expenses in Vietnam.

Despite backing from the Americans, France's ability to continue the fight was weakening. The French failed to win the popular support of the Vietnamese people, and most remained staunchly behind Ho Chi Minh and the independence movement. The Vietminh also received considerable financial and military support from China and the Soviet Union.

With the conflict at a stalemate, the Chinese and Soviets pressured Ho Chi Minh to seek a peace settlement. To that end, a conference convened in Geneva, Switzerland, on April 26, 1954. But before the talks could begin, the French military in Vietnam would suffer a humbling defeat.

Disaster at Dien Bien Phu

Few westerners had ever heard of Dien Bien Phu—meaning "Principal Frontier Post"—until the First Indochina War. The French considered it to be one of the most strategically important places in French Indochina, and in 1953 had launched an airborne assault to capture it from the Vietminh.

The French commander, Henri-Eugene Navarre, wanted Dien Bien Phu to be the centerpiece of a classic set-piece battle. In such a battle, the armies of both sides are arrayed in opposing battle formations. He brought all available artillery to Dien Bien Phu, and built strong fortifications. Navarre hoped to wipe out Giap's forces as they launched futile assaults against his impregnable fortress at Dien Bien Phu.

By the end of 1953, 20 infantry and artillery battalions, totalling about 15,000 men, were stationed at Dien Bien Phu. Navarre placed the stronghold under the command of Colonel Christian de la Croix de Castries, a cavalry officer known for his dash and courage. The French believed they were ready for the battle to begin. However, things did not play out according to General Navarre's plan.

The Vietnamese commander General Giap saw through Navarre's strategy. He opted not to attack right away at Dien Bien Phu. Instead, he ordered a series of diversionary attacks in Laos and elsewhere in Vietnam. These attacks drew French support away from Dien Bien Phu. The Vietminh guerrillas then stealthily withdrew from the other fronts.

Vietnamese troops charge the French fortifications at Dien Bien Phu, May 1954. The fall of the fort to the Vietminh ended French hopes of maintaining control over its colony in Southeast Asia.

During the first quarter of 1954, Giap massed four divisions in the hills around Dien Bien Phu and ringed the fortress with 200 artillery pieces.

On March 13, 1954, Giap launched his assault under cover of a thunderous artillery barrage. Bursting shells soon ravaged French defensive positions and rendered its two airstrips inoperable. Within a few weeks, monsoon rains washed out the fort's three access roads. Supplies for the French garrison had to be air-dropped into the besieged fort.

With each passing day, some 50,000 Vietminh soldiers tightened the ring around Dien Bien Phu. They moved slowly but relentlessly toward the French fortress, digging trenches by hand. On May 1, General Giap began his final assault on the fortress. Overrunning one position after another, Giap's forces finally broke through French defenses on May 7. By day's end, the long battle had ended. Eleven thousand French survivors laid down their arms. With the fall of Dien Bien Phu, France lost much of its bargaining strength at Geneva—and, by extension, its rule in Indochina.

In Washington, a State Department memorandum expressed U.S. fears that a negotiated settlement "would mean the eventual loss to Communism not only of Indo-China but of the whole of Southeast Asia." It concluded: "If the French actually decided to withdraw, the U.S. would have to consider most seriously whether to take over in this area." The fear of communist expansion expressed in the memo had already begun to shape U.S. foreign policy. Even as France took leave of Indochina, U.S. policymakers were inching toward a deeper American involvement in Vietnam.

 TEXT-DEPENDENT QUESTIONS

1. What is communism?
2. What three kingdoms make up the modern state of Vietnam?
3. What 1940 event did Ho Chi Minh want to use to advance the cause of Vietnamese independence?

 RESEARCH PROJECT

Communism is a political system in which the government (the state) controls all of the country's resources and factories. Explain how this is different from the system in the United States today.

Chapter 2

An Unpopular Regime in South Vietnam

During the Cold War, U.S. leaders subscribed to the *domino theory*. This theory held that if one nation should fall under a communist government, neighboring countries would soon follow suit. U.S. President Dwight D. Eisenhower explained this theory during a press conference on April 7, 1954. "You have a row of dominoes set up," Eisenhower said, "you knock over the first one, and what will happen to the last one is the certainty that it will go over very quickly." This kind of thinking laid the foundation for U.S. involvement in Vietnam in the years following France's departure.

U.S. president Dwight Eisenhower and secretary of state John Foster Dulles greet South Vietnamese president Ngo Dinh Diem on his arrival in the United States, 1957. The Eisenhower administration supported Diem's government in South Vietnam, despite its refusal to hold democratic elections and the repressive tactics of its secret police.

In the spring of 1954, a peace conference was held in Geneva, Switzerland, for the purpose of resolving the conflict in Indochina, as well as in Korea where a war had been fought from 1950 to 1953. At Geneva, an agreement ended the First Indochina War and divided Vietnam into two zones at the 17th parallel. Like Korea, the two zones were to be separated by a temporary *demarcation* line called a demilitarized zone (DMZ). A Final Declaration issued on July 21, 1954, called for free elections to be held throughout Vietnam in July 1956.

However, neither the state of South Vietnam nor the United States agreed to this Final Declaration. President Eisenhower recognized that the communists in North Vietnam would surely win that election by virtue of the northern zone's population advantage of several million. To thwart a communist victory at the polls, the Eisenhower administration decided to support Emperor Bao Dai's anticommunist regime in the south.

In July 1954, before the close of the Geneva Conference, Bao Dai had called on nationalist Ngo Dinh Diem to create a new government in South Vietnam. Diem was a strong anticommunist and a devout Roman Catholic. He had ties to the West, having lived and been educated in the United States and Belgium. Although the French distrusted Diem, he had the support of the United States. Diem formed a new government for the

 WORDS TO UNDERSTAND IN THIS CHAPTER

autocrat—a ruler who has absolute power.

coup—a sudden, violent, and illegal seizure of power from a government.

demarcation—to fix a boundary or border.

domino theory—the idea that a communist takeover in one country will cause similar communist takeovers in neighboring countries, like a falling domino causing an entire row of dominoes to fall.

referendum—a general vote by citizens on a political question that has been referred to them for a direct decision.

Vietcong—a contraction of *Viet Nam Cong San*, meaning "Vietnamese communist." This term was used for South Vietnamese who waged a guerrilla war against the U.S.-supported regime.

French-supported South Vietnam zone, becoming prime minister.

The Geneva Accords said that the Vietnamese people could choose whether they wanted to live under the North's communist government, or in the southern zone. Diem's position in South Vietnam was strengthened by the arrival of nearly 1 million refugees from the communist north. Many of them were Roman Catholics, who predominantly supported Diem.

Diem took further steps to consolidate power in South Vietnam during the spring of 1955, when he launched military operations against several political opponents. One was the Cao Dai religious sect, which had an army of around 25,000 that had been established around 1943 to oppose Japanese occupation. Diem's forces also attacked the

Vietnamese refugees prepare to board an American warship, USS Montague, *at Haiphong. Of the approximately 1 million Vietnamese who fled to the South, more than 300,000 were transported by the U.S. Navy during Operation Passage to Freedom in 1954-55. Many were Catholics who feared religious persecution by the communist government.*

Buddhist Hoa Hao, which also had a small (about 2,000) private army, and the Binh Xuyen, a criminal organization that was involved in drug dealing, prostitution, and gambling. The French had paid these gangsters to fight against the Vietminh in South Vietnamese cities. Diem justified the attacks by accusing the groups of harboring communists.

In October 1955, Diem called for a national *referendum* to decide whether the country should become a republic under his leadership as president or continue under the rule of Bao Dai. Diem officially won more than 98 percent of the vote, though most experts believe the elections were rigged.

This map of Vietnam shows the division of the country at the 17th parallel.

On October 26, Diem declared that the southern zone would become the Republic of Vietnam, with himself as president. U.S. secretary of state John Foster Dulles announced that the United States would send economic and military aid, as well as advisers, to South Vietnam to help Diem's government. In November 1955, the U.S. Military Assistance Advisory Group–Vietnam (MAAG) was formed, and U.S. aid began pouring into South Vietnam.

Although the United States supported Diem, its leaders recognized that he was an *autocrat*, not a democratic leader. The U.S. looked the other way when Diem refused to hold open, fair elections in the South.

North Vietnam's communist allies, the Soviet Union and Communist China, did not press the issue of free elections. They did not want to set a precedent for similar elections in the partitioned nations of Germany and Korea, where most of the population resided in the noncommunist zones. Meanwhile, Ho Chi Minh, frustrated by his inability to gain Vietnamese unity by political means, decided on a different approach.

An Insurgency in the South

Although Vietnamese were permitted to move to the zone they supported after the cease-fire in 1955, many Vietminh had decided to remain in South Vietnam. Just because a person had fought with the Vietminh against the French did not mean he was against Diem, or supported the communist North. However, Diem's forces harassed and attacked anyone with a Vietminh connection. This drove many people to oppose Diem.

In late December 1956, Ho Chi Minh asked Vietminh living in the South who opposed the Diem regime to begin insurgency operations against the Diem regime. During 1957, the cadre organized 37 armed companies in the Mekong Delta. Insurgents assassinated more than 400 minor South Vietnamese officials.

The insurgents succeed in part because of Diem's unpopularity. The president's policies had alienated the Buddhists in a country where most of the people were Buddhists. His policies favored landowners in a land of peasants. Diem overturned land reforms that had been enacted by the Vietminh during World War II, and he took land from peasants and gave it back to the landowning class. Diem further distanced himself from the people by replacing locally elected provincial chiefs with his own political appointees, many of whom were family members. And he suppressed critics who denounced his regime for corruption and lack of reform by imprisoning and torturing them. His brother, Ngô Dình Nhu, was in charge of the secret police, which became feared for its brutality.

The Vietnam War Begins

By January of 1959, the situation in South Vietnam had become so bad that Ho Chi Minh felt pressured to go to war, even though he did not believe North Vietnam was ready. His deputy Le Duan argued that if communists didn't lead now, as resistance to Diem was beginning, they would become irrelevant in the struggle. At a meeting in Hanoi, the Central Executive Committee of the Communist Party issued Resolution 15—a directive changing the communist strategy from "political struggle" to "armed struggle." Scholars generally believe that the issuance of Resolution 15 marked the start of the Second Indochina War, now known to Americans as the Vietnam War.

The Vietminh veterans who had been waging the insurgency in the South formed the nucleus of the National Liberation Front (NLF). Diem's public relations staff gave these rebels the unflattering label of *Vietcong*, a contraction of Viet Nam Cong San, meaning "Vietnamese communist." The name stuck.

In May of 1959, North Vietnam began enlarging the Ho Chi Minh Trail, the vital supply line for the Vietcong in the South. The trail started

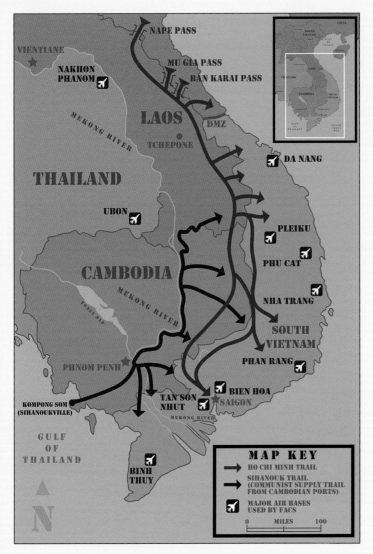

This map shows the route of the Ho Chi Minh Trail, the major supply line for the Vietcong in South Vietnam. The trail ran through jungle areas in neighboring Laos and Cambodia, where the North Vietnamese Army and Vietcong established bases and training camps from which to launch attacks on military and political targets in South Vietnam.

in North Vietnam, wound through Laos and Cambodia, and forked off into various destinations in South Vietnam. By July, a continuous stream of men, guns, munitions, food, and medical supplies began to flow southward to support the "armed struggle" declared by Hanoi.

On July 8, 1959, the Vietcong staged an attack at Bien Hoa and killed two U.S. military advisers—Major Dale Buis and Master Sergeant Chester Ovnand. They were the first two Americans to die in the Vietnam War. Thousands more would follow. The war between the two Vietnams heated up in the summer of 1959. Overall, things went well for the North. By the end of 1960, the Vietcong controlled vast areas of the Mekong Delta, the Central Highlands, and the Coastal Plains.

In November 1960, South Vietnamese army troops tried to overthrow Diem's government in Saigon. Diem survived the attempted *coup* and retained power, despite his growing unpopularity. Diem's position grew even more critical in 1961 as Vietcong attacks increased in size and effectiveness. The weight of Diem's worsening situation in Vietnam fell heavily on the new U.S. president, John F. Kennedy, as he took office in January 1961.

A New Direction

By the end of President Eisenhower's second term in office, the United States had invested hundreds of millions of dollars in an effort to build a new nation in South Vietnam. Before leaving office, Eisenhower assured Ngo Dinh Diem, "The United States will continue to assist [South] Vietnam in the difficult yet hopeful struggle ahead." Eisenhower hoped his vow would bind his successors to his policies.

In November 1960, John F. Kennedy had defeated Richard Nixon to win the presidency. At Kennedy's inauguration in January 1961, the incoming president made it clear that his administration would continue to stand firm against communism. "Let every nation know, whether it wishes us well or ill," Kennedy announced, "that we shall pay any price, bear any burden, meet any hardship, support any friend, oppose any foe, in order to assure the survival and the success of liberty."

Over the next 22 months, the number of U.S. advisers sent to South Vietnam increased from about 900 in early 1961 to roughly 16,300 by November 1963. Even so, communist successes in the South continued. President Diem refused to act on some of the recommendations of U.S. advisers, and he continued to suppress opposing

President John F. Kennedy followed the foreign-policy lead of his predecessors, subscribing to the "domino theory" and seeking to contain communism through the use of military advisers and counterinsurgency tactics in Vietnam.

political and religious factions. Anti-Diem demonstrations became commonplace.

In May 1963, South Vietnamese troops and police fired on Buddhists celebrating a festival in the city of Hué. The crisis escalated in June. To protest Diem's policies, a Buddhist monk doused himself with gasoline and was set afire at a busy Saigon intersection.

By this time, U.S. leaders recognized that Diem and his administration were hampering, not helping, the U.S. goal of containing communism in Southeast Asia. On November 1, 1963, a group of South Vietnamese generals stormed the presidential palace in Saigon. Ngo Dinh Diem and his brother fled but were caught the next day and shot. Although the United States did not take an active role in the planning or execution of the coup, it went forward with Washington's tacit approval.

 TEXT-DEPENDENT QUESTIONS

1. Where was the 1954 conference to resolve conflicts in Asia held?
2. What line of latitude was used to divide North Vietnam from South Vietnam?
3. What was the name of the group that waged an insurgency against the government of South Vietnam?

 RESEARCH PROJECT

The AK-47 was the primary weapon used by the Vietcong during the Vietnam War. It was also commonly used by other military forces supported by the Soviet Union. Do some research on this type of firearm. What was the range, and how accurate were these weapons? Were there any limitations or drawbacks to using them? Why were they so popular among communist-supported guerrillas? Write a one-page report on what you learn.

Chapter 3

America Increases its Involvement

After the overthrow and assassination of Diem in Saigon, political analysts predicted that the coup would force Washington to take a more active part in the country's government. It would also, they said, draw the United States more deeply into prosecuting the war. The analysts were right on both counts.

Nobody can say for sure what path America might have followed in Vietnam had President John F. Kennedy lived, but Kennedy was assassinated in Dallas

President Lyndon B. Johnson (1908–1973) greets American soldiers in South Vietnam during a visit to the military installation at Cam Ranh Bay in October 1966. During Johnson's term in office (1963–1969), the U.S. commitment of troops in Vietnam increased sharply. The unpopularity of the Vietnam War caused Johnson to decide not to seek reelection in 1968.

just a few weeks later. Many experts believe Kennedy would not have tried to *extricate* the United States from its commitments in South Vietnam until at least after the presidential election of 1964. However, the question of what do about America's involvement in the tiny Asian nation now belonged to Kennedy's successor, vice president Lyndon Baines Johnson.

Johnson, popularly known as "LBJ," was a career politician who had aspired to the highest office in the land for most of his adult life. He took office bent on doing nothing, either at home or abroad, that might harm his chances of retaining the presidency on his own in the 1964 election. The last thing he wanted to do was to look weak in the face of communist expansionism. LBJ remembered how critics had soundly denounced President Truman for "losing China" after the communist takeover there in 1949. He had no wish to invite similar criticism for "losing" Vietnam.

Like his predecessors, President Johnson readily accepted the domino theory and the need to contain communism. In December 1963, the U.S. Joint Chiefs of Staff (JCS) began preparing a series of tough military options to counter Hanoi's operations in South Vietnam. They planned to present them formally to the new president in January 1964. These options included air strikes and commando actions against North Vietnam. They also recommended *reconnaissance* flights over Laos and Cambodia. Further, if necessary, they proposed the introduction of regular U.S. combat forces. Above all, the JCS considered it essential for a U.S. commander to take charge of the actual direction of the war. In short, they wanted to turn Vietnam into an American venture.

In January 1964, Secretary of Defense Robert S. McNamara selected Lieutenant General William C. Westmoreland to serve as deputy commander of the U.S. Military Assistance Command Vietnam (MACV).

 WORDS TO UNDERSTAND IN THIS CHAPTER

extricate—to free someone or something from a constraint or difficulty.
reconnaissance—military observation of a region to locate an enemy
   or ascertain strategic features.

General William C. Westmoreland, commander of U.S. forces in Vietnam from 1964 to 1968, speaks to television reporters outside the White House. Westmoreland conducted a war of attrition and became widely known for his "search-and-destroy" brand of warfare. To the left is U.S. Secretary of State Dean Rusk, who consistently defended the U.S. role in Vietnam and became a target of antiwar protests.

Westmoreland was a distinguished veteran of World War II and the Korean War. He would soon become a household name in America on the televised nightly news. At month's end, General Nguyen Khanh seized power in South Vietnam from General Minh, who had led the coup against Diem.

By February 1964, it was clear that the South Vietnamese government was losing ground fast in its battle against the Vietcong. President Johnson ordered the withdrawal of American civilians from the region. Two months later, Hanoi ordered North Vietnamese regular army units to begin slipping into South Vietnam. About 10,000 North Vietnamese Army (NVA) troops crossed into South Vietnam in 1964, representing another communist escalation that President Johnson could not ignore.

By mid-1964, President Johnson had inaugurated secret talks with North Vietnam aimed at halting the war in the South. The United States offered economic aid and diplomatic recognition as an incentive. Hanoi insisted on the withdrawal of U.S. forces and Vietcong participation in a neutral South Vietnamese government. Those talks would remain stalemated for the next 10 years.

The Gulf of Tonkin Incident

With South Vietnam teetering on the edge of collapse, Washington desperately needed a reason to widen the war. Also, LBJ needed some way to counter the criticisms of Senator Barry Goldwater of Arizona, his ultra-

This painting depicts the August 2, 1964, engagement between the USS Maddox *and three North Vietnamese motor torpedo boats in the Gulf of Tonkin.*

conservative Republican rival for the presidency. Goldwater was criticizing Johnson's handling of the deteriorating situation in Vietnam for his "no-win" policy and was calling for an expansion of the war. In early August, a curious affair in the Gulf of Tonkin provided both LBJ and his administration with just what they needed.

On August 2, 1964, North Vietnamese torpedo boats attacked the U.S. destroyer *Maddox*, which was on a reconnaissance mission in the Gulf of Tonkin. Hanoi acknowledged the attack, claiming the *Maddox* had violated its territorial waters. Secretary of Defense McNamara later called the attack "unprovoked" while the U.S. destroyer was "on routine patrol in international waters." Earlier that day, South Vietnamese patrol boats had attacked North Vietnamese shore facilities, which may have triggered the attack on the *Maddox*. In any case, after repelling its attackers, the *Maddox* retreated down the gulf.

Two days later, on August 4, the *Maddox* returned to the scene of the original incident with a second U.S. destroyer, the *Turner Joy*, to establish a U.S. presence. Amid murky circumstances, a second attack on the two destroyers allegedly occurred, although no physical evidence—photographs or battle damage—substantiated the attack.

On August 4, 1964, President Johnson addressed the nation in a special late-night telecast: "It is my duty to the American people to report that renewed hostile actions against United States ships on the high seas in the Gulf of Tonkin have today required me to order the military forces of the United States to take action in reply." Even as he spoke, U.S. carrier-based planes were winging toward North Vietnamese naval installations and storage facilities for a retaliatory air strike.

On August 10, the U.S. Congress passed the Gulf of Tonkin Resolution. It authorized the president to "take all necessary measures to repel any armed attack against the forces of the United States and to prevent further aggression."

Several months after the curious happenings in the Gulf of Tonkin, President Johnson reportedly said, "For all I know, our Navy was shoot-

President Johnson signs the Joint Resolution for the Maintenance of Peace and Security in Southeast Asia, better known as the "Gulf of Tonkin Resolution," at the White House, August 10, 1964. The resolution gave Johnson the authority to send American combat troops to Vietnam.

ing at whales out there." Critics of LBJ cite this seemingly flippant remark as evidence of a deliberate attempt to deceive the American public by the president and his administration. LBJ's defenders insist that he and his advisers did not knowingly lie about the attacks. Although they were clearly in a mood to strike back, they got caught up in a morass of conflicting reports from the gulf. They were guilty only of selecting the evidence that best suited their aims. Whichever view is true, the violence in Vietnam continued to escalate. Johnson easily defeated Goldwater in the November election, and America moved a step closer to all-out war.

Escalation of the War

By the end of 1964, the number of U.S. military personnel in Vietnam had grown to 23,300, while South Vietnamese armed forces stood at an increased strength of some 514,000. Meanwhile, Vietcong attacks in the south grew stronger and more audacious, while men and supplies continued to pour south along the Ho Chi Minh Trail from North Vietnam.

An American tank on patrol in Saigon.

U.S. Air Force F-105 jets drop their bombs on targets in North Vietnam as part of Operation Rolling Thunder.

On February 7, 1965, the Vietcong attacked U.S. installations at Pleiku and Qui Nhon. In retaliation, the United States launched air strikes against the southern panhandle of North Vietnam in February. And in March, U.S. air operations over North Vietnam commenced in earnest. Code-named Operation Rolling Thunder, the air operations were authorized and closely controlled by President Johnson. Over the next three years, U.S. aircraft dropped some 643,000 tons of bombs on North Vietnamese targets, while losing 922 aircraft to enemy action.

Rolling Thunder's air attacks on North Vietnam provoked increased Vietcong attacks on American air bases in South Vietnam. On February 22, 1965, General William C. Westmoreland requested two marine battalions to protect the U.S. air base at Da Nang. He said later that he had not then seen his request as the "first step in a growing American commitment" in Vietnam. Most Americans had not seen it that way either at the time.

On March 8, 1965, the Third Marine Regiment of the Third Marine Division—about 3,500 men—splashed ashore at Da Nang. Within a month, the mission of U.S. troops had changed, however. U.S. soldiers were no longer just protecting air bases, but actively fighting the Vietcong. Ground troops were sent on offensive operations, although patrols were limited to a 50-mile radius from American coastal bases.

Additional marine and army units quickly followed and began offensive "search and destroy" operations in June. In September, General Vo Nguyen Giap launched a major offensive in the Central Highlands, south of Pleiku. Westmoreland responded with the First Air Cavalry Division. November 1965 saw fierce fighting in the Ia Drang Valley, as American and North Vietnamese troops clashed in force for the first time.

By the end of the year, U.S. troop strength in Vietnam had reached almost 200,000. All pretenses as to America's "advisory" role in South Vietnam went by the boards. America was openly at war in Asia. In December 1965, French journalist and author Bernard B. Fall prophetically remarked, "The incredible thing about Vietnam is that the worst is yet to come." American leaders were not listening.

 TEXT-DEPENDENT QUESTIONS

1. What American general commanded U.S. forces in Vietnam from 1964 to 1968?
2. What was the name of the U.S. warship involved in the Gulf of Tonkin incident?
3. How many tons of bombs were dropped by U.S. aircraft during Operation Rolling Thunder?

 RESEARCH PROJECT

Go to http://vietvet.org/letters.htm to read some letters written during the Vietnam War by American soldiers. What are some similarities between the letters? What are some of the differences?

Chapter 4

The American Way

I n 1966, President Johnson continued to pour U.S. troops into Vietnam, as General Westmoreland pursued aggressive actions in a war of *attrition* against the North Vietnamese and Vietcong. America's industrial strength and technology enable its massive use of firepower and "high-tech" weaponry. Analysts often label it "the American way of war."

Attrition became the primary U.S. military strategy during the Vietnam War. General Westmoreland demanded a strict accounting of enemy dead from his

Young men who have been drafted wait in line to be processed into the U.S. Army at Fort Jackson, South Carolina.

field commanders. This led inevitably to the notorious "body count," a grisly means of measuring the success of U.S. forces. Since the performance of military commanders was judged by the numbers of enemy soldiers his men killed, the temptation to inflate the figures became an unsurprising possibility. Both civilian and combatant corpses were sometimes counted as certifiable bodies. These grim practices contributed to U.S. attacks on South Vietnamese villages later in the war.

The numbers of enemy dead were tabulated, reported to Washington, D.C., and released to the media by U.S. authorities. Body counts of enemy dead became featured highlights on the evening television news. Television's stark depiction of warfare in the raw soon turned off American viewers. Westmoreland later charged that "television's unique requirements contributed to a distorted view of the war." Given TV's very nature, he argued, "the news had to be compressed and visually dramatic, and as a result the war that Americans saw was almost exclusively violent, miserable, or controversial." Critics of television went further yet, claiming that TV coverage lost the war in Vietnam. In the meantime, the war surged on.

During the first full year of America's involvement in Vietnam, U.S. forces conducted a series of operations against North Vietnamese regulars and the Vietcong. Each operation was given a name: Van Buren, Masher/White Wing, Paul Revere, Utah, Texas, and so on, to name a few. President Johnson, complaining to military top brass in Honolulu in 1966, said, "I don't know who names your operations, but 'Masher.' I get

 WORDS TO UNDERSTAND IN THIS CHAPTER

attrition—the wearing down of an enemy force by killing or disabling its soldiers. It seeks to destroy not only the enemy's armed forces but also its will to resist.

defoliant—a chemical that removes the leaves from trees and plants. It is used during jungle warfare to make it harder for enemy soldiers to conceal themselves.

U.S. Secretary of Defense Robert McNamara points to a map of Vietnam during a press conference. McNamara was one of the chief architects of America's military policies in Vietnam. Early in the war McNamara believed that American technological superiority would guarantee victory. By 1966, he had privately begun to doubt that the war could be won.

kind of mashed myself." Thereafter, officials added "White Wing," presumably to lessen the harsh-sounding effect. But America's rush into to war kept on escalating. By the end of 1966, troop levels reached 385,000. And American dead totaled 6,644 to date.

The following year, Westmoreland launched massive combat strikes in a big push to find and annihilate the Vietcong and North Vietnamese regulars. He called upon his staff to create "expressive terms" to indicate operations "designed to find, fix in place, and destroy . . . enemy forces and their base areas and supply caches." His staff obliged, coining the phrase "search and destroy." The brutality implied by the phrase, along with vivid television images of Vietnamese villages being destroyed, helped undermine public support for the war.

While attrition served as the basic American strategy in Vietnam, U.S. forces employed various tactics to achieve the desired end. (Strategy is the planning and directing of the entire operation of a campaign or war, whereas tactics is the art of placing or maneuvering forces skillfully in a battle.)

One major development in American tactics introduced the use of helicopters to move troops into battle positions. This tactic is often referred to as an airmobile operation. The forested terrain of Vietnam dictated another major change to American tactics. Conventionally, fire power generated by artillery and close air support is used to fix an enemy in place. Maneuvering infantry units would then move into position and destroy the enemy with attacks on its flanks and rear. Vietnam's forest-limited visibility forced U.S. forces to reverse the process. Infantry units would first find the enemy unit, then call in artillery and air strikes to eliminate it.

Westmoreland's search-and-destroy tactic exemplified this approach. This tactic was meant to be used with two others: "clearing" operations and "securing" operations. Clearing operations were aimed at driving

An American UH-1B helicopter brings supplies to a unit of the Fourth Infantry Division that is engaged in a search and destroy mission near Dak To, December 1967. Due to the jungle terrain, helicopters were needed to move and resupply American troops in the field.

ARVN troops charge into action against the Vietcong in the Mekong Delta region.

enemy units from populated areas in preparation for pacification. (MACV defined pacification as "the military, political, economic, and social process of establishing or re-establishing local government responsive to and involving the participation of the people.") Securing operations were used to protect pacification troops, eliminate remaining local guerrillas, and "uproot the enemy's secret political infrastructure."

An alternative approach—the enclave strategy—called for U.S forces to occupy major population centers and coastal bases in a defensive posture. It was advocated by General Maxwell Taylor, ambassador and military advisor, who contended it would free the Army of the Republic of Vietnam (ARVN) to bear the brunt of the fighting against the North Vietnamese and Vietcong. Both General Westmoreland and the top military leaders in Washington favored "taking the battle to the enemy." As a result, the enclave approach was relegated to "fallback" role whenever the American war seemed to be faltering or at a stalemate.

AGENT ORANGE

One innovation peculiar to America's war in Vietnam began to gain notoriety during the late 1960s. A *defoliant* named Agent Orange was used to deprive enemy fighters of cover and supplies. Approved for use by President Kennedy in 1961, it was introduced into Vietnam in 1962. Agent Orange was an herbicide containing minute amounts of a deadly toxin known as dioxin. It was sprayed from specially equipped C-123 transport planes, as well as other aircraft. Nearly 850,000 acres of forests and crops were destroyed by chemical herbicides in 1966 alone. By 1967, 1.5 million acres a year was being destroyed by Agent Orange. Sprayings in Vietnam were terminated in 1971.

By eliminating trees and bushes where enemy forces could hide, defoliation undoubtedly saved the lives of many American soldiers. At the same time, it produced unanticipated casualties of war. Beginning in the late 1970s, Vietnam veterans began to cite dioxin as the cause of a variety of health problems. Their maladies ranged from skin rashes to cancer to birth defects in their children.

Veterans started filing claims against Agent Orange-induced disorders to the Department of Veterans Affairs (VA) in 1977. The VA initially denied most claims, but today recognizes "certain cancers and other health problems as presumptive diseases associated with exposure to Agent Orange or other herbicides during military service." Vietnam veterans who develop these diseases, or their survivors, may be eligible for payments or health care from the government.

An American UH-1D helicopter sprays Agent Orange on a dense jungle area in the Mekong delta.

North Vietnam's strategy in the war was both simple and effective. Ho Chi Minh and General Vo Nguyen Giap executed the same three-phase plan that had worked so well against the French: (1) they built support bases and focused on survival; (2) they initiated guerrilla activities, using small groups of fighters behind enemy lines to place booby traps and conduct small ambushes; and (3) they first placed major reliance on "political struggle," then reverted to "armed struggle" to strike a decisive blow against South Vietnam.

Americans Turn Against the War

By the end of 1967, American troop strength in Vietnam totaled about 485,600. The total of American dead stood at 16,021. In the United States, students and war dissenters were taking to the streets in violent protest against the increasingly unpopular war.

The turning point in the Vietnam War came soon after the Tet Offensive in late January 1968. Named for a Vietnamese holiday celebrating the start of the lunar new year on January 30, the Vietcong/North Vietnamese offensive featured a series of coordinated attacks against urban centers and military installations across South Vietnam. U.S. and South Vietnamese forces repulsed the attacks everywhere and achieved a resounding military victory over the Vietcong and North Vietnamese. But strategically, politically, and psychologically, Hanoi gained an even greater victory when the Tet offensive convinced many war-weary Americans that the war could not be won. Public opinion soon turned against remaining in Vietnam.

As early as 1967, Secretary of Defense Robert S. McNamara had recognized the failure of U.S policies—largely of his own making—toward the war in Vietnam. He announced his resignation in November and left office on February 29, 1968. President Johnson appointed Clark Clifford, a suave elder statesman, as McNamara's replacement.

Counter to Westmoreland's search-and-destroy approach to the war, Clifford recommended an alternative policy to the president. "Perhaps we should not be trying to protect all of the countryside," he said, "and instead concentrate on the cities and important areas in the country." Johnson, like McNamara before him, finally conceded that there could be

Vietnamese civilians cross the Perfume River to escape fighting in Hué during the Tet Offensive. The battle for Hué was one of the longest and bloodiest of the war. The North Vietnamese Army and Vietcong surprised the American and South Vietnamese defenders when Tet began, and captured the city. It took a month of intense urban fighting before the Americans and South Vietnamese could recapture the city.

no military solution in Vietnam. A new kind of war was taking shape.

On the day that Clifford took office, the Tet Offensive ended. In its wake, General Westmoreland assessed the military situation in Vietnam. He recognized that from a military standpoint, the United States and its allies had dealt a severe blow to the communists. Sensing that his enemy stood on the verge of military collapse, he requested additional troops from Washington. He wanted to bolster his forces for a final knockout blow against the North Vietnamese. But Americans largely interpreted the general's call for additional troops as confirmation that the war was going badly in Vietnam.

In reality, the Joint Chiefs of Staff had urged Westmoreland to request more troops for reasons of their own. They meant to use the war in Vietnam as an excuse to activate reserve forces and rebuild the nation's reserve pool for use in potential encounters in places other than Vietnam. The public—not privy, of course, to the inner workings of the military and Washington—kept the pressure on America's leaders to end the war.

The Fighting Intensifies

While anti-war demonstrators took to the streets in America, some of the war's fiercest fighting took place in the spring of 1968. General Westmoreland's headquarters reported some 3,700 Americans killed and

U.S. Marines fire on enemy positions from their base at Khe Sanh.

another 18,000 wounded, against an estimated 41,000 communist dead.

Beginning on January 21 and continuing beyond the end of the Tet Offensive, the North Vietnamese assault on the U.S. Marine base at Khe Sanh stretched into one of the war's most controversial battles. Upgraded by Westmoreland in the summer of 1967, it was one of a series of combat bases and strong points paralleling the DMZ along Route 9. Khe Sanh formed the westernmost anchor of the line, close to the Ho Chi Minh Trail near the Laos border. Westmoreland intended to interdict the Ho Chi Minh Trail and move into Laos using Khe Sanh as a launch point.

Set in a valley and surrounded by mountains, Khe Sanh's vulnerability invited numerous comparisons to the ill-fated French bastion at Dien Bien Phu. Such comparisons were later refuted by a North Vietnamese officer interviewed by journalist Stanley Karnow. "At Dien Bien Phu, the French and ourselves massed for what we both expected to be a final battle," the NV officer told Karnow. "The Americans were strong everywhere in the south. Thus we realized from the beginning that we could not beat them decisively in a single encounter like Khe Sanh." Neither could they defeat the U.S. Marines in the siege of Khe Sanh.

Battling tenaciously, the marine defenders at Khe Sanh fought off their NVA attackers for eleven weeks. By the time the siege was lifted on April 7, some 1,602 North Vietnamese lay dead on the battlefield. Overall, General Westmoreland estimated that the North Vietnamese lost somewhere between 10,000 and 15,000 men. U.S. Marine Corps dead totaled 205. Ironically, plans to interdict the Ho Chi Minh Trail failed to win approval in Washington, D.C. Khe Sanh was evacuated and abandoned in June 1968. It was the American way of war.

 TEXT-DEPENDENT QUESTIONS

1. How many U.S. troops were in Vietnam by the end of 1966?
2. What U.S. general advocated the enclave strategy?
3. What event in early 1968 turned American public opinion against the Vietnam War?

 RESEARCH PROJECT

During the Vietnam War era (1958-1973), the U.S. government held a military draft. Young Americans between the ages of 18 and 25 had to register for the draft, and each year a certain number were randomly chosen to serve in the armed forces. Soldiers were drafted to fill vacancies in the military that could not be filled by volunteers alone, but as the number of American soldiers in Vietnam increased, so did the need for more draftees. Using the Internet or your school library, find out more about the military draft. Write a report providing statistics and information about the draft and whether it was effective.

Chapter 5

Peace with Honor

While the U.S. Marines clung to their bastion at Khe Sanh, the seemingly endless war in Vietnam affected President Johnson deeply. In a televised address on March 31, 1968, Johnson announced that he would restrict the bombing of North Vietnam and pursue a negotiated peace settlement with Hanoi. He ended his address with a stunning revelation. "I have concluded," he said solemnly, "that I should not permit the presidency to become involved in the partisan divisions that are developing in this political year. . . .

As the number of American casualties in Vietnam grew, so did the peace movement in the United States. By 1968, antiwar marches and demonstrations were becoming common, as Americans began to question the purpose of fighting a war in Southeast Asia.

Lyndon B. Johnson addresses the nation in March 1968, announcing a bombing halt in Vietnam and his intention not to run for re-election in that fall's presidential election.

Accordingly, I shall not seek, and I will not accept, the nomination of my party for another term as your president."

Hanoi announced its willingness to talk with the Americans three days after President Johnson's dramatic peace gesture. Peace talks commenced in Paris on May 13 but soon led nowhere. The communist high command insisted that U.S. bombings (which were still partially in progress) must be halted before serious negotiations could begin.

A New Plan to Win the War

In June 1968, General Creighton W. Abrams succeeded General Westmoreland as MACV commander. Abrams faced the difficult task of executing the disparate policies of the outgoing Johnson administration and those of his yet-to-be-determined successor.

On October 31, 1968, President Lyndon B. Johnson announced a complete halt to the bombing of North Vietnam, ending the U.S. Air Force's Operation Rolling Thunder. The bombing cessation failed to revitalize peace talks, however. A period of bickering between the U.S. and its South Vietnamese allies ensued.

In November 1968, Richard M. Nixon defeated Hubert H. Humphrey in the presidential election. Americans elected him partly on his promise of a secret plan to bring "peace with honor" to Vietnam. In private, Nixon

 WORDS TO UNDERSTAND IN THIS CHAPTER

matériel—military materials and equipment.
quagmire—a problematic situation that is hard to get out of.

also declared, "I will not become the first president of the United States to lose a war."

Nixon's plan called for an increase in U.S. artillery and aerial bombardments, while building up South Vietnam's armed forces and *matériel*. As South Vietnam assumed more and more responsibility for the war, U.S. forces were to be gradually withdrawn. Secretary of Defense Melvin Laird later summed up the plan as "Vietnamization," and the name stuck.

It should be noted that the troop reduction had already begun during the Johnson administration. U.S. troop strength in Vietnam had peaked at 585,000 shortly after the Tet Offensive in early 1968. By the end of 1968, the number of American troops in Vietnam had fallen to 536,100.

By the time President Nixon took office in January 1969, both the U.S. Congress and the American people had turned irrevocably against the

Although Nixon had promised to end the Vietnam War, more bombs were dropped and more American soldiers killed during his administration than under the administration of President Johnson.

The U.S. Air Force bombed key points on the Ho Chi Minh Trail in Laos, such as the bridges pictured in this aerial photo. Numerous bomb craters can be seen along the trail, which passed through the mountains and jungles of the Laotian panhandle.

war. The first substantive peace talks began in Paris on January 29. Despite Nixon's peace efforts, the immensely unpopular war was destined to grind on for another seven years.

In mid-March, Nixon initiated a secret bombing campaign. To gain maneuvering room for U.S. troop withdrawals, he authorized bombings to a depth of five miles within neutral Cambodia. B-52 bombers destroyed North Vietnamese base camps in the border areas that had been used as launch points for raids into South Vietnam. The Nixon administration kept the bombing campaign secret from Congress and the American public for two years. Operation Menu succeeded only in driving the North Vietnamese deeper into Cambodia.

During May 8–20, a fierce battle for Hill 937 (Ap Bia Mountain) in the A Shau Valley cost the lives of some 241 American soldiers. Reports of the fighting for "Hamburger Hill," provoked widespread unfavorable publicity in the United States. The hill was named from the fact that the battle turned into a "meat grinder."

Nixon's Peace Overtures

On May 14, President Nixon proposed an eight-point peace plan for Vietnam, providing for mutual troop withdrawal. Hanoi rejected it and countered with its own plan—which in turn was rejected by the U.S.—and the diplomatic dance began anew.

Washington warned Hanoi that its delay in reaching a peace agreement might result in the carpet bombing of its cities, the mining of its harbors, and possibly the spread of radioactive debris to halt its infiltration of the South. At the same time, Nixon cultivated improved relations with the Soviets and Chinese to better solicit their help in pressuring Hanoi to come to terms.

Nixon, in a conversation with White House aide Bob Haldeman, explained, "I want the North Vietnamese to believe I've reached the point where I might do anything to end the war." He called his threats the "madman theory." Neither deeds nor threats produced any immediate concessions from Hanoi. In June, in an effort to show that the U.S. commitment to the war was winding down, Nixon ordered an immediate withdrawal of 25,000 troops from Vietnam.

On July 25, 1969, President Nixon announced a new policy for U.S. support of allied nations threatened with external attack. He reaffirmed that the U.S. would honor its treaty commitments. It would continue to provide a nuclear shield and provide military and economic assistance as appropriate. He added that going forward "we shall look to the nation directly threatened to assume the primary responsibility of providing the manpower for its defense." In other words, South Vietnam's military would have to take a greater role in the war, with U.S. troops gradually being withdrawn. At the same time, Nixon stepped up the air war. Journalists dubbed the new policy the "Nixon Doctrine."

Nixon's new policy provided a path for America to exit from what had become a *quagmire*, while still achieving his promise of an "honorable peace." At year's end, Nixon promised a further withdrawal of 50,000 troops by mid-April 1970.

Attacks on Cambodia and Laos

In the spring of 1970, as American troop withdrawals continued, Nixon ordered a "limited" invasion of Cambodia to demonstrate continued support for the South Vietnamese. The Cambodian incursion failed to sever North Vietnamese supply lines as planned. Actually, it accomplished little other than to buy additional time for Vietnamization. On the down side, it added fuel to a revitalized antiwar movement in the United States. A firestorm of protests erupted across the nation, culminating in the deaths of student protesters at Kent State University and Jackson State University.

On May 8, Nixon tried to dampen the flames of protest, announcing that all U.S. troops would be completely withdrawn from Cambodia by

President Nixon points out NVA sanctuaries along the Cambodian border in his speech to the American people announcing the Cambodian incursion, April 30, 1970.

July 1. In a news conference, he insisted that "at the same time we are cleaning out the enemy sanctuaries in Cambodia, we will pursue the path of peace at the negotiating table [in Paris]."

In January 1971, in an effort to show that South Vietnamese troops were ready to fight on the own, Nixon sanctioned an offensive into Laos (Lam Son 719) using only ARVN troops. Their attempt to sever the Ho Chi Minh Trail failed. The ARVN withdrew within six weeks, with the communist supply route still intact. The botched incursion served little more than to stiffen the president's resolve. Some feel it may also have contributed to his harsh response to the release of the *Pentagon Papers* on June 13, 1971.

The *Pentagon Papers* (officially *The History of the U.S. Decision Making Process on Vietnam*) consisted of secret documents detailing the role of the United States in Indochina and Vietnam from World War II to 1968. Daniel Ellsberg, a hawk-turned-activist, released them to *The New York Times*.

Outraged Americans perceived the *Pentagon Papers* as evidence of government deception on the conduct of the war. Release of the Papers prompted Nixon to create a White House unit to plug leaks of information to journalists. The cover-up of its illegal activities—collectively known as the Watergate scandal—would later lead to President Nixon's resignation in 1974.

Vietnamese Air Force crewmen line up before one of the 62 UH-1 "Huey" helicopters turned over to them November 4, 1970, along with command of the Soc Trang airfield, as part of Nixon's "Vietnamization" strategy.

North Vietnam Takes the Offensive

In the spring of 1972, after four years of stalemated peace efforts, North Vietnam launched what became known as the Eastertide Offensive on March 30. It proved to be one of its major miscalculations of the war. Hoping to take advantage of the U.S. troop withdrawals, North Vietnam committed an entire army with tanks and artillery to a cross-border three-pronged attack against ARVN units in Quang Tri, Kontum, and An Loc.

South Vietnamese forces—aided by massive U.S. artillery support, B-52 bombers, and other Navy and Marine aircraft—repelled the invaders with heavy losses. The ARVN defenders killed an estimated 100,000 enemy troops and destroyed at least one-half of their large-caliber

A B-52 drops its bombs on North Vietnam. The massive 1972 bombing campaign known as Linebacker II forced the North Vietnamese to resume negotiations on a peace agreement that would allow the United States to withdrawal from Vietnam.

artillery and tanks. Additionally, B-52 bombers and Navy mine-laying aircraft mined and closed North Vietnamese ports to oceangoing traffic. American bombers further destroyed ten MiG bases, six major power plants, and all large oil storage facilities in North Vietnam.

Peace talks were suspended in March 1972, but resumed in the late fall. They soon faltered again when South Vietnamese President Nguyen Van Thieu could not agree to a truce. Nixon secretly promised Thieu that the U.S. would recommit troops to South Vietnam if North Vietnam broke the truce. When the North balked at a revised proposal already agreed to, Nixon lost all patience. He summoned Chairman of the Joint Chiefs of Staff Admiral Thomas Moorer to Camp David and told him, "This is your chance to use military power effectively to win the war, and if you don't, I'll consider you responsible."

On December 17, 1972, President Nixon ordered Operation Linebacker II, also known as the "Christmas Bombing." On December 18, the U.S. launched an all-out air campaign against the Hanoi area. For eleven straight days, Air Force fighter-bombers from bases in Thailand, Navy fighter-bombers off carriers, and a fierce concentration of B-52 strategic bombers rained death and destruction on the North Vietnamese capital. They dropped 36 tons of bombs.

To stop the bombing, North Vietnam agreed to return to the negotiating table. Both sides had finally wearied after long years of war. Representatives of North Vietnam and the United States agreed on terms for a peace settlement.

A Peace Settlement

On January 27, 1973, representatives of the United States, South Vietnam, North Vietnam, and the Vietcong signed a peace agreement in Paris. Nixon characterized the settlement as "peace with honor." Critics viewed it differently, pointing out that it merely allowed U.S. military forces to withdraw from the conflict without resolving the political future of South Vietnam.

Without the U.S. military, South Vietnam would soon cease to exist. In the spring of 1975, North Vietnam launched a Spring Offensive, drove all the way to Saigon, and forcibly integrated South Vietnam into the Democratic Republic of Vietnam.

U.S. Secretary of State William P. Rogers signs the Peace Agreement ending the Vietnam War, January 27, 1973.

A section of the Vietnam Veterans Memorial in Washington, D.C. The black granite memorial, often referred to as "the Wall," lists the names of more than 58,250 Americans who were killed during the Vietnam War.

In 1985, in his book *No More Vietnams*, Nixon defended his Vietnam policies. "In the end," he argued, "Vietnam was lost on the political front in the United States, not on the battlefront in Southeast Asia." He firmly believed that his numerous escalations in the war—far from being a useless waste of lives—had shortened the conflict.

America's war in Vietnam claimed the lives of more than 58,000 American soldiers, with more than 153,000 others wounded in battle. Vietnamese losses, both North and South, were infinitely higher. It is believed that more than 3 million Vietnamese soldiers and civilians were killed during the conflict.

The Vietnam War had long-lasting consequences for the United States. The conflict weakened U.S. military morale and made American leaders wary of becoming drawn into conflicts in other parts of the world. Since the 1970s, the American public's aversion to casualties has led military leaders to attempt to minimize the use of ground troops, instead relying heavily on air power to project American military might. Equally important, the war made many Americans deeply suspicious of government.

Most military and political experts agree that the Vietnam War was a tragic event whose costs far exceeded America's gains. The United States tried to curb communism in Vietnam and create a nation in its own image without regard to the history and culture of the Vietnamese. The American military won many battles in the field, but American leaders failed on the political, diplomatic, and cultural fronts.

 TEXT-DEPENDENT QUESTIONS

1. What general succeeded Westmoreland as commander of American forces in Vietnam?
2. What secret U.S. Department of Defense documents were leaked to the *New York Times* in 1971, providing information about American activities in Cambodia and Laos?
3. What was Linebacker II?

 RESEARCH PROJECT

Using the Internet or your school library, find out more about the Vietnam Veterans Memorial. Who came up with the idea for the Vietnam Veterans Memorial? Where is it located? Who designed the memorial? When was it dedicated? How does the design reflect the American experience in the Vietnam War? Write a two-page paper on the Memorial, and share it with your class.

Chronology

1941   Ho Chi Minh forms the League for Vietnamese Independence (Vietminh). World War II begins.

1945   Vietminh collaborate with the U.S. Office of Strategic Services (OSS) in guerrilla warfare against the Japanese. World War II ends.

1946   Democratic Republic of Vietnam established. First Indochina War begins.

1950   President Truman authorizes $15 million in military aid to the French in Indochina; U.S. supplies $1 billion in aid to French military efforts in Indochina by 1954.

1953   French paratroopers seize Vietminh command post at Dien Bien Phu in November.

1954   Vietminh General Vo Nguyen Giap launches an assault on Dien Bien Phu in March; French-held fortress falls on May 7, marking the end of the First Indochina War.

1955   Geneva Accords divide Vietnam into two military zones in July and call for free elections throughout Vietnam a year later. Republic of Vietnam founded in December. Ngo Nguyen Diem elected president.

1957   Vietminh begin low-level insurgency operations in the Mekong Delta.

1959   Hanoi changes communist strategy from "political struggle" to "armed struggle."

1960   National Liberation Front (NLF; popularly known as Vietcong) formed in Hanoi. John F. Kennedy elected U.S. president. Outgoing President Dwight D. Eisenhower pledges continued support for South Vietnam.

1963   American military advisers in Vietnam increase from 900 in

1961 to 16,300. Presidents Ngo Nguyen Diem and John F. Kennedy assassinated. Vice President Lyndon B. Johnson accedes to the U.S. presidency.

1964   General William C. Westmoreland takes command of MACV in South Vietnam. North Vietnamese patrol boats attack U.S. destroyers in the Gulf of Tonkin. U.S. Congress passes Gulf of Tonkin Resolution (Public Law 88-408).

1965   Vietcong attack U.S. installations in South Vietnam in February. Operation Rolling Thunder begins in March. Third Marine Regiment lands at Da Nang in April. U.S. troop levels in Vietnam reaches 200,000 by year's end.

1966   Westmoreland conducts war of attrition. Body counts mount. U.S. troop strength in Vietnam climbs to 385,000.

1967   U.S. forces in Vietnam reach 485,000. Westmoreland launches massive "search and destroy" operations. War protesters take to the streets in the U.S.

1968   Communists launch Tet Offensive, marking the war's turning point. U.S. public opinion begins to turn against the war. General Creighton W. Abrams succeeds General Westmoreland as MACV commander. U.S. troop strength in Vietnam peaks at 585,000. Long period of troop reduction begins. Richard M. Nixon, promising a "secret plan" to end the war in Vietnam, is elected president.

1973   Representatives of the U.S., South Vietnam, North Vietnam, and the Vietcong sign peace agreement in Paris on January 27. U.S. forces withdraw from Vietnam.

1975   North Vietnam launches Spring Offensive and reunifies Vietnam as a communist nation. Saigon renamed as Ho Chi Minh City.

Chapter Notes

p. 11   "The best organized ..." Ho Chi Minh, quoted in William H. Duiker, *Ho Chi Minh: A Life* (New York: Hyperion, 2000), p. 160.

p. 12   "The French defeat represents ..." Ibid.

p. 12   "Between the enemy and ourselves ..." Ibid.

p. 14   "We are convinced that the Allied nations ..." Ibid.

p. 15   "I order all soldiers and militia ..." Ibid.

p. 20   "would mean the eventual loss ..." U.S. State Department memo, quoted in *Advice and Support: The Early Years, 1941-1960* (Hawaii: University Press of the Pacific, 2005), p. 176.

p. 20   "If the French actually decided ..." Ibid.

p. 21   "You have a row of dominoes ..." Dwight D. Eisenhower, quoted in James H. Willbanks, *Vietnam War: The Essential Reference Guide* (Santa Barbara, Calif.: ABC-CLIO, 2013), p. 49.

p. 27   "The United States will continue ..." Dwight D. Eisenhower, quoted in Larry Berman, *Planning A Tragedy: The Americanization of the War in Vietnam* (New York: W.W. Norton, 1982), p. 15.

p. 27   "Let every nation know ..." John F. Kennedy, Inaugural Address, January 20, 1961. http://www.jfklibrary.org/Research/Research-Aids/Ready-Reference/JFK-Quotations/Inaugural-Address.aspx

p. 33   "It is my duty to the American people ..." Lyndon B. Johnson, "Radio and Television Report to the American People Following Renewed Aggression in the Gulf of Tonkin," August 4, 1964. http://www.presidency.ucsb.edu/ws/?pid=26418

p. 33   "take all necessary measures ..." Tonkin Gulf Resolution. Public Law 88-408, 88th Congress, August 7, 1964; General Records of the United States Government; Record Group 11; National Archives.

p. 33   "For all I know ..." Lyndon B. Johnson, quoted in Robert D. Schulzinger, *A Time for War: The United States and Vietnam, 1941-1975* (New York: Oxford University Press, 1997), p. 151.

p. 35   "first step in a growing American commitment" William C. Westmoreland, quoted in Berman, *Planning a Tragedy*, p. 52.

p. 36   "The incredible thing about Vietnam ..." Bernard B. Fall, "This Isn't Munich, It's Spain," *Ramparts* (December 1965), p. 28.

p. 38   "television's unique requirements contributed ..." William C. Westmoreland, *A Soldier Reports* (New York: Dell, 1980), p. 150.

p. 38   "the news had to be compressed ..." Ibid.

p. 39   "designed to find, fix in place ..." William C. Westmoreland, quoted in Gregory A. Daddis, *No Sure Victory: Measuring U.S. Army Effectiveness and Progress in the Vietnam War* (New York: Oxford University Press, 2011), p. 100.

p. 43   "Perhaps we should not ..." Clark Clifford, quoted in notes of meeting with President Lyndon B. Johnson, March 4, 1968. U.S. State Department Archive. http://2001-2009.state.gov/r/pa/ho/frus/johnsonlb/vi/13695.htm

p. 45   "At Dien Bien Phu ..." quoted in Stanley Karnow, *Vietnam: A History* (New York: Viking, 1991), p. 542.

p. 47   "I have concluded that I ..." Lyndon B. Johnson, "Address to the Nation Announcing Steps To Limit the War in Vietnam and Reporting His Decision Not To Seek Reelection," March 31, 1968. http://www.lbjlib.utexas.edu/johnson/archives.hom/speeches.hom/680331.asp

p. 49   "I will not become ..." Richard M. Nixon, quoted in J. Edward Lee and H.C. "Toby" Haynsworth, *Nixon, Ford and the Abandonment of South Vietnam* (Jefferson, NC: McFarlane & Co, 2002), p. 28.

p. 51   "I want the North Vietnamese ..." Richard M. Nixon, quoted in H. R.Haldeman, *The Ends of Power* (New York: Times Books, 1978), p. 122.

p. 51   "we shall look to the nation ..." Richard M. Nixon, "Address to the Nation on the War in Vietnam," November 3, 1969. http://www.presidency.ucsb.edu/ws/?pid=2303

p. 52   "at the same time we are ..." Richard M. Nixon, transcript of news conference, May 8, 1970. http://www.presidency.ucsb.edu/ws/?pid=2496

p. 54   "This is your chance to use ..." Richard M. Nixon, quoted in Willbanks, *Vietnam War*, p. 171.

p. 56   "In the end, Vietnam was lost ..." Richard M. Nixon, *No More Vietnams* (New York: Arbor House, 1985), p. 45.

Further Reading

Appy, Christian G. *Patriots: The Vietnam War Remembered from All Sides*. New York: Viking Penguin, 2004.

Brownell, Richard. *America's Failure in Vietnam*. Farmington Hills, MI: Lucent Books/Gale Group, 2005.

Gibson, Karen. *The Vietnam War*. Hockessin, DE: Mitchell Lane Publishers, 2007.

Hamill, Pete. *Vietnam, the Real War: A Photographic History by the Associated Press*. New York: Abrams, 2013.

Karnow, Stanley. *Vietnam: A History*. Revised and updated. New York: Viking, 1991.

Wagner, Heather Lehr. *Henry Kissinger: Ending the Vietnam War*. New York: Chelsea House Publishers, 2007.

Internet Resources

http://www.army.mil/cmh-pg/html/bookshelves/collect/vn-studies.html
The official website of the U.S. Army provides an exhaustive study of U.S. Army operations in all phases of the Vietnam War.

http://www.eagleton.rutgers.edu/research/americanhistory/ap_vietnam.php
This website of the Eagleton Institute of Politics of Rutgers, the State University of New Jersey, contains a detailed examination of the Vietnam War and list of additional resources and educational tools.

http://www.pbs.org/wgbh/amex/vietnam/index.html
Website for the Public Broadcasting System's series "The American Experience: Vietnam Online," an online companion to "Vietnam: An Online Television History."

http://www.vietnam.ttu.edu/
The Vietnam Center and Archive at Texas Tech provides information and documents about the various Indochina Wars and collects and electronically publishes oral histories and memoirs of both those who served in and those who opposed those conflicts.

Index

Numbers in **bold italics** refer to captions.

SERIES GLOSSARY

blockade—an effort to cut off supplies, war material, or communications by a particular area, by force or the threat of force.

guerrilla warfare—a type of warfare in which a small group of combatants, such as armed civilians, use hit-and-run tactics to fight a larger and less mobile traditional army. The purpose is to weaken an enemy's strength through small skirmishes, rather than fighting pitched battles where the guerrillas would be at a disadvantage.

intelligence—the analysis of information collected from various sources in order to provide guidance and direction to military commanders.

logistics—the planning and execution of movements by military forces, and the supply of those forces.

salient—a pocket or bulge in a fortified line or battle line that projects into enemy territory.

siege—a military blockade of a city or fortress, with the intent of conquering it at a later stage.

tactics—the science and art of organizing a military force, and the techniques for using military units and their weapons to defeat an enemy in battle.